Freeing Space in
Your Home, Office, & Mind

by

Cynthia Lee De Boer

Freeing Space in Your Home, Office & Mind

Written by Cynthia Lee De Boer

Edited by Toni Briegel
Cover design by James Kelly & Cynthia De Boer

Published by
OpenHeart Press
PO Box 50014
Las Vegas, Nevada 89014

www.cynthialdeboer.com

ISBN: 978-1-7321384-6-9
Copyright © 2020

All rights reserved including the right of reproduction in whole or in part in any format, digital or physical.

INTRODUCTION

My name is Cynthia Lee De Boer. I'm an author, speaker, and disability advocate. I am also the former owner of Harmony Organizational Consulting & Cleaning. Through this business, I was able to help my clients take control of their space and their time. It was life changing for them and gratifying for me. Being an organized person has always been important because of my sight issues and this need has helped me serve others. I invite you to take this journey to freedom with me and discover how much time you will gain to enjoy your life. You will discover what motivates us to hold on to belongings, how to be true to your personal needs and desires and how to respectfully downsize into freedom.

"How can you see all the beauty in your life when you're busy taking care of all the things you own? I believe clutter is keeping too many of us from living well. Let's change that."
~ Erica Layne

THE EMOTIONAL SIDE

Life is full of things that can be frustrating or take up unnecessary time. Our belongings should not fall into these categories. Living an organized and uncluttered life allows us to spend our time wisely instead of wasting it caring for things we do not use, like, or need. If you think about it, most of us use a very small percentage of the items we accumulate. You will discover that freeing space in your home, office, and mind is worth the effort. Grasping and understanding this process will make it easier to downsize to the items that serve the greatest purpose and make you the happiest. In the end, decluttering means fewer items to keep up with which, in turn, equals less stress.

"Clutter is not just the stuff on your floor—it's anything that stands between you and the life you want to be living."
~ Peter Walsh

Let's begin by answering the following questions. You may want to write these down along with your answers. Putting the questions in your own handwriting makes the experience more relevant.

1. Why have your decided to take on this project?
2. What is your purpose?
3. Are your belongings getting out of control?
4. Is it hard to find what you're looking for?
5. Are you downsizing to a smaller home or office?
6. Has your lifestyle or needs changed?
7. Do you feel overwhelmed—as if your things own you?
8. Is financing your items causing you stress?
9. Are you spending too much time cleaning, caring for, or working to support your belongings?
10. And finally, what result do you want? Your WHY is your purpose, keeping it in the forefront of your mind will help you stay on track. *Minimizing* belongings *maximizes* our free time. After all, time is the only commodity we cannot replace. How do you want to spend yours?

"Less stuff equals more freedom."
~ Maxime Legace

Next, we need to understand a few of the reasons we keep things. The emotions that often drive our decision-making are *fear*, *guilt, regret, respect* and even *insecurity*. We fear we will need an item in the future, even though that likelihood is remote. Others fear that they may not have the funds to repurchase something if they toss it. This is especially true for anyone that has lived through hard times. Often this will lead to a person hoarding things whether they are stained, broken, or will never be used. In that person's mind, the "never used" items are things to barter with for more possessions they do need.

These **fears** can be difficult to address. It is probably best to ignore this issue until you've experienced success and freedom in other areas. At that time, you can then ask yourself, "What's the worst that can happen without owning that item?" If it is something like a garden tool or even a steam cleaner, you might consider borrowing it from a friend. In all likelihood, it's not going to be so vital that if you don't purchase it, it will be a life changing event.

There are times when you may inherit a piece of furniture or be gifted something you just don't want. You may experience feelings of **guilt** about getting rid of those items. No one wants to hurt loved ones or friends. However, I believe that if someone truly cares for you, they will not want a gift to cause you stress. Perhaps it would be easier to simply express your appreciation for their thoughtfulness and explain that the item doesn't fit your lifestyle. If you don't want to offer it back to them, you could re-gift it to someone you think would enjoy it or donate it to charity.

Then there is the **guilt** of wasting money on something that you no longer like or need. Maybe you've grown tired of collecting dolls or stuffed animals. This is especially true if the collectables are expensive or were a gift. Again, consider offering it back to the giver. If not, passing collectables on to others who share a common interest is a great idea. Alternatively, simply donate them to a worthy cause. This will make you feel good in having given to others with a similar interest, and it will help to combat that feeling of **guilt**.

Regret enters the scene when addressing hobbies or projects that we may have started but never completed. These are "someday projects" often viewed as "life unlived" and you feel you have to keep. Eliminating them from your live frees you from self-prescribed obligation. However, if one of the reasons you're freeing space is to create time for a project, then by all means get rid of the nonessential clutter and establish a sufficient area to work on your project. Make it a "today project."

Insecurity is another emotion that can take over our lives. The desire to keep up with the Jones and even surpass them, will propel people into an endless cycle of buy, buy, buy. When we constantly view our own self-worth by what we own, or in most cases have a loan on, is a form of **insecurity**. We, ourselves, are enough without the having lavish possessions. The following quote sums this up.

"Too many people spend money they haven't earned; to buy things they don't want, to impress people they don't like."
~ Will Rogers & Will Smith

Respect yourself by altering your perspectives on downsizing. Stop viewing the process as being difficult and be grateful for all you have. Take charge of your space and time. View your belongings with fondness and relish your ability to pass along those you don't need to others.

Respect is a vital part of this process. Everyone is on an individual path. Others in your life may not understand your decisions. If you find it necessary, express your reasons and explain your plan for achieving your desired outcome. Know that you may hit some resistance, but again this is about you. Remember your *Why* and stick to your plan. You may also be amazed that the changes you make may help someone else see the benefits of freeing space in their lives. It's also important to let others know that just because you've freed space in your area, it's not for them to use. This is a common problem, and you must be clear by setting and sticking to the boundaries you set. It's frustrating to clear a space only to find someone has taken it over. Keep in mind, just because you've decided to free space in your home, office, and mind, doesn't mean everyone else has arrived at that same decision.

Before we begin this process, I wish to share a story about a friend of mine from England. As we were riding through my neighborhood, she noticed several cars in each driveway. She asked me how many vehicles most people own. I answered that when a couple lives in a home, they usually own two cars because generally they both work outside the home.

She followed up that question by asking me, "Why are both cars parked in the driveway, why not the garage?" I replied that the garages are often full of overflow from their homes and/or things stored for future garage sales.

Her next comment was so true and brought home what I've felt for years. She commented that it makes no sense that a vehicle costing tens of thousands of dollars is left outside in the elements, while a few hundred dollars of discarded items are kept safely inside.

Think about what you may have taking up precious space, while important things are not being cared for properly.

"The ability to simplify means to eliminate the unnecessary so that the necessary may speak."
~ Hans Hofmann

THE PROCESS

No matter what category you're working through, some basic steps should be followed along with a few specific requirements for each.

Emotional items should always be done last. You need to experience the process in order to understand how good it will feel to be free of things you no longer want or need.

1. Truly feeling grateful for your home and belongings is a positive way to begin this journey.
2. Most of us utilize a very small percentage of our belongings, no matter what they are. Realizing this helps when discarding and organizing. It also allows space for easier access to items we do use.
3. Use the available space to decide what to keep. Simply put, if it doesn't fit, it doesn't stay.
4. Make a commitment to yourself and your space to downsize first, then clean, and finally, organize.
5. Imagine the space you want. Taking a current photo may help you decide how you want

things to look. Before and after photos help us see our progress and keep us on track.
6. Remember, you didn't collect your belongings in a day and sorting through them will take time. Decide on the amount of time you have to devote to each category and stick to it. Be generous when scheduling your time as it may take longer than you initially believe.
7. Sort by categories not locations. In other words, sort all your clothes at the same time, no matter where they are located. By piling up all the things in each category you will most likely be surprised by how much you own. This will help you understand how much you do not use, need, or even like.
8. Your area will become more of a mess at the beginning; but take heart—it will be well worth it. The satisfaction and pride of a job well done is incredible.
9. Have bags or boxes available to donate, return to others, or toss.
10. Follow this order: Clothes, Books, Paper, and Miscellaneous items including kitchen, electronics, and tools. The last area is sentimental and may include items from several categories. If so, place them together for later. Taking photos of sentimental things and placing them in a *Memory Book* is a great way to enjoy those things without having to

own them. This is perfect for any downsizing project.
11. Remember to thank each item for its service before discarding it and only keep what makes you feel good or is necessary for your lifestyle.
12. Remove any discards or donations as quickly as possible so you don't second guess yourself.
13. Rolling towels, bedding, and other items placed in cabinets or on shelves is a nice way to display and easily access your belongings.
14. Drawers, bins, or boxes may be used to separate like items. Store them vertically to allow you to see what you own. When things are placed one on top of the other, this is not possible.
15. Place seldom-used things in harder-to-reach places, while keeping the easily reached areas for those frequently used.
16. Make sure to organize and store by size. Give everything a home. For instance, small items of the same category can be kept together.
17. When possible, you may decide to arrange by color.
18. Use containers you can see into or label those you cannot.
19. Labeling also helps keep belongings in order with many preferring to label shelves—even in their refrigerators.
20. When the process is complete it's important to consistently purge items that don't make you

happy, are no longer used or needed. And always return things to their homes.

"Any job well done that has been carried out by a person who is fully dedicated is always a source of inspiration."
~ Carlos Ghosn

FREEING SPACE & ORGANIZING EACH CATEGORY

CATEGORY #1—CLOTHING

Clothing can get out of hand. Too many sales, impulse buys, or gifts that aren't our style simply pile up. Unfortunately, these items suffocate the things we do want to wear. Most of us utilize a small fraction of our clothing. The process of sorting through these belongings may seem a bit crazy, but I want you to view your items with gratitude. Put on soothing or uplifting music, have a favorite beverage at hand, and begin with a smile and gratitude for all you have. You'll get through this and feel so much better when it's done. First, designate an area for your clothes as you sort them. Mark bags or boxes as RETURN, DONATE, TOSS, and KEEP. Next, place every item of clothing you own on your bed no matter where it is in your home. Again, we are sorting by category and not location.

By doing this, you will be able to see everything you own. The large number of items we own is a surprise most of us. The purpose of this is to realize how blessed we are. Getting rid of things you don't wear doesn't mean you can't obtain or replace worn out clothes in the future. Look at what you have accumulated. Looking at a mound of clothes on the bed can be daunting, but if you focus on the end result, it will be much easier. The reality is you probably don't wear the majority of what's stacked up.

Begin by holding each item up and acknowledging how it makes you feel. If you feel good when you wear it, it's a keeper. If it doesn't have that effect on you, determine why. Is it the wrong size, just doesn't fit well, isn't your style, or is the item torn or stained? Once you've made your decision, place it in the appropriate area as RETURN, DONATE, TOSS, or KEEP. Personalize it. Be sure to thank the item for its service as you release it.

Once you have finished sorting, gather the clothing in the assigned piles and distribute the ones you no longer desire as soon as possible. This eliminates second-guessing. It is imperative that once you've made your decision to stick with it.

You will find that releasing your unwanted wardrobe will make it easier to access what you decide to keep. Next, let's organize. Seasonal, holiday, special occasion, and clothing that doesn't currently fit should be stored at the back of the closet or drawer, thereby giving easy access to the items you wear daily. If you're losing or trying to gain weight, I suggest that you only keep a few of your favorite items that you might fit into after the weight change. Turn the new you into a celebration. Purchasing something new to wear is a delight. You could even display an item of clothing as inspiration to help you achieve your goal. If you are an expectant mother, you probably should hold off on sorting through your clothes.

It's a good idea to hang like-clothes together. The following are groups of outfits you probably own: t-shirts, shirts and blouses, dress pants, jeans, suits, dresses, work clothes, seasonal outfits, special occasion, and clothing for future weight changes. You may also have specific clothes you use for exercise, hobbies, or clubs. By keeping like items together, you are creating sections that make it easy to locate what you want in an instant.

Arrange each section by sleeve length and then by color, light to dark, or the reverse. This is your space, so do what works best for you. If you prefer to fold some of these items, that's okay. We'll get to folding in a bit. Scarves can also be folded, rolled, or placed on hangers.

Going forward, one way to see what you truly wear and help to continue your freeing journey is to place all your hangers in a backward position. Then, after an item is worn and laundered, place it on a hanger in the normal direction. After a few months, check to see what clothes are unworn on the backward hangers. Consider discarding them, as they are only taking up unnecessary space in your closet.

Jackets, Coats, Sweaters, Hats, & Gloves: I wear scarves with some of my outerwear and prefer to keep them together on the same hanger. I also suggest that when possible, keep outerwear in a coat closet or separate from your other clothes. Outer wear collects pollens, dust and sometimes moisture. Placing them by themselves will keep your other belongings cleaner. Downsize to what fits your lifestyle and makes you happy.

Shoes, Bags, & Wallets: Shoes, bags, and wallets wear out, become uncomfortable, or no longer fit a person's needs. Be honest with yourself by keeping only the things that fit your current lifestyle. Once you have decided what you're keeping, decide on a storage method. Many people prefer to have their shoes and bags on shelves and, as long as you can access them easily, that's fine. However, if they are on high and hard-to-reach shelves or under clothes on the floor, the chances of using them or even knowing what you have decreases. If boxes are your preferred storage method, use clear or labeled boxes to make it easy to locate what you need. Boxes are available in several sizes from shoebox size on up to very large sizes. Larger sizes work well for boots or allow you to place several like-things together in one box. Once again, make them easy to access. You can always put a folding step stool in your closet to help with high shelves.

Folding Clothes: When clothes are folded and then layered one on top of the other, the only way to know what's in the drawer or box is by rummaging through them. This makes a mess of the organized wardrobe.

I suggest placing your folded clothes in a vertical position, one behind the other like pages in a file. In this way, you can see everything and arrange them by color. You can use this method with everything in your dresser drawers.

The club t-shirts my husband wears have graphic designs on the back. I fold them with the graphic designs on the outside so they can be seen when they are placed in his drawer. In this manner, he can choose the exact shirt he wants at a glance, instead of having to unfold several to locate the preferred one. Graphics should be visible no matter what side of the shirt they're on. Remember, the goal is to make life easier.

NOTES

- Replacing mismatched hangers with like hangers and using matching boxes or bags give your closet a refined and fresh look.
- Hang all clothes on hangers placed backwards until worn so you can actually see what you wear as this helps keep you on track in the future.
- Remove plastic dry cleaning bags from clothing to prevent moisture build up.
- An inexpensive full-length mirror is a great addition to your closet or any area where you dress.
- A folding step stool may be necessary to reach high shelves. If you cannot reach it, you're not going to use it.

CATEGORY #2—BOOKS

Gather all your books and magazines and create a pile for each. When sorting is complete, decide how you would like to organize them. Here are a few ideas: by genre, by color, in alphabetical order by title or author's name, or by height on the shelf. Whether you choose one, or combine a few methods, the choice is yours. Make it fit your needs and design style.

CATEGORY #3—PAPER

Some papers may not make us smile, but they are necessary to keep. These may include tax documents, receipts, birth and marriage certificates, home deeds, and other legal paperwork. It's important to keep these documents safe and secure from identity theft. A lock box, safe, or safety deposit box are methods preferred by most. Choose what works for you. Warranties should be kept where you can easily access them. Outdated statements and any paperwork that is no longer needed, but contains personal information, should be shredded before it's discarded. Any remaining paperwork may be scanned into your computer so you can shred or toss the hard copies. If you decide to take this approach, make sure to back up your information in case your computer fails.

Wrapping paper, bags, bows, and gift cards also fall into this category. It's best to store these things together in a decorative bin or box.

CATEGORY #4—MISCELLANEOUS ITEMS

Now it's time to tackle your kitchen, electronics, entertainment items, hobbies, fitness equipment, and things stored in the garage. This is a very broad category and can be organized following the method as everything else.

Kitchen: Gather all kitchen supplies, gadgets, and machines together and decide what you actually use. Next, place the less used items in the harder to reach areas, and keep those most frequently used in the easily accessible areas. When doing so, it's important to keep the needs of others in mind. If there are children in the house, or someone in a wheelchair, or someone with a height issue, designating a lower shelf or cabinet is wonderful. This includes snacks, cups, bowls, plates, and utensils. Allowing them to have more independence frees you from having to assist them. Independence from others decreases and eliminates stress. It's a win-win for everyone. Cleaners and poisonous chemicals should be kept out of a child's reach, and safety latches should be installed where necessary.

Electronics & Entertainment: Once again, these items should be placed where they are used. Discard plastic cases or cardboard containers you will never use again. After you have sorted cords, chargers, CD's and DVD's, you can save space by and placing them in organized bins or boxes.

Hobbies & Fitness: Arrange these items in a way that allows you to access them more easily, based on use. Many of us have "someday hobbies." These are items you may have purchased on a whim. Perhaps your life or desires have changed. This is normal, but now it's time to pass these along for someone else to experience.

Miscellaneous Tools: Tools and supplies for working on our homes, vehicles and hobbies should be gathered, sorted, and placed where they are needed the most.

NOTES
Garages are often the dumping ground for unwanted or unused items. I hope that this process has categorized and sorted much of what lives there. If not, do so now.

CATEGORY #5—SENTIMENTAL

This final category is often the most difficult to deal with. Hopefully, your success up to now will help you take this next step with confidence and gratitude. The biggest problem most people face when they downsize is the loss of their treasured things. Personal items hold memories and may cause you to grieve when you think about giving them away. Many of these possessions are often stored in boxes in the garage or at the back of a closet. Frankly, we rarely see or enjoy them. A great way to hold on to those memories is by taking photos and placing them in a *Memory Book* with a caption or story that can be easily accessed and enjoyed. An alternative would be to display those special belongings in a shadow box as artwork on your wall. This allows you to enjoy those items year-round. Hidden belongings are never enjoyed, they just take up space.

MORE TIPS

Plastics: Some people, like me, are looking for ways to eliminate plastic from their lives. We all lived without plastics for years and now it seems everything is made of it, from kitchenware to bins, boxes, bags, and even trashcans. I give my plastics to people who want and can use them, or I recycle them to avoid a landfill. I resist buying anything plastic, but, sadly, many wrappers are plastic, and I haven't found a solution for avoiding that. The cost for natural options can be equal to or greater than the plastic we're trying to replace. Take it one item at a time and think about the appropriate substitution. For instance, I use items made from glass, metal, wood, cloth, and cardboard. The type of material depends on the intended purpose and needed location.

Open Shelving: I love open shelving and it helps many maintain a simple lifestyle. My warning is to use it only in areas you know you can keep neat. A messy or cluttered shelf looks just as bad as an untidy workspace.

Double-Duty Items: Here are a few items you may find helpful around the house.

Consider placing rubber bands around hangers to hold spaghetti strap blouses and dresses from falling off hangers. Shower rings can be daisy-chained over a hanger to hold scarves. Metal clips can be placed on wire racks to hold back water and soda bottles. Paper towel racks can be used for bracelets. Shower caps can be used to cover shoes in suitcases to keep clothes clean. Staple removers can be used to open key rings. Clear nail polish can be used to keep tiny screws in eyeglasses. Placing tall bottles in boots can help them stay upright. New clean dental floss can be used to cut cakes, breads and other pastries.

"I wish you the best in your next adventure of Freeing Yourself."
~ Cynthia Lee De Boer

About the Author

This "how-to" book, *Freeing Space in Your Home, Office, & Mind*, was created to help the reader understand that freeing oneself from unused or unwanted possessions allows more time for the important things in life.

Cynthia's mission is to help people change their perspectives on disabilities and depression by speaking about her life lessons and thereby letting others know they are not alone.

Cynthia Lee De Boer's career as an author, inspirational speaker, and disability advocate is fueled by her medical challenges, relationships, and work experiences.

Her first book *Me, Myself & Eye, The Realities of Living with a Prosthetic Eye* has been widely received as an honest and much-needed resource. Cynthia donates a portion of the proceeds from this book to the NFB (National Federation of the Blind).

Her second book, *Freedom From Depression, No Matter What Your Disability May Be,* was developed from her speaking engagements and is a comprehensive guide designed to help the reader implement the changes necessary to create a happier life. Cynthia believes having a disability does not make you less of a person, it makes you more of a human being.

Her third work is a children's book titled *Jimmy's Magic Turtle*. This wonderfully illustrated two-line rhyme story was written to celebrate children who imagine "What if." A portion of the proceeds from each book sold will be donated to The Marfan Foundation in honour of her nephew, Jimmy.

Website: www.cynthialdeboer.com
Email: c.deboerauthorspeaker@gmail.com
Facebook:
https://www.facebook.com/cynthia.deboer.73
Instagram:
https://www.instagram.com/cynthialeedeboer/?hl=en

www.ingramcontent.com/pod-product-compliance
Lightning Source LLC
Chambersburg PA
CBHW070859050426
42453CB00012B/2270